How to Get Over a Breakup – Forever!

A 9-Step Strategy Guide to Stop Feeling
Sad and Get Over Your Ex

B. L. HALLISON

ISBN: 1519694784
ISBN-13: 978-1519694782

DEDICATED TO
THE READER

May you discover the empowerment and
acceptance of different relationships closing and
new ones beginning.

TABLE OF CONTENTS

INTRODUCTION

Have you ever been in love or had a special connection with one particular person? Has it ever not gone the way you had anticipated?

Unfortunately, most people will have to go through several romantic partners until they find the person they settle with – which can involve several heavy and difficult romantic break-ups.

It is not uncommon during a break up to feel uncontrollably angry or sad, or a myriad of other powerful and unwanted emotions. However, this guide exists to aid you dealing with the emotional process – what kind of emotions you can expect, how you should interpret them, and how to move forward.

In particular, this guide offers practical advice: learn how to really *feel* your feelings, accept your own individual journey and develop your unique coping methods. Explore the underlying nature of the most stormy and tricky emotions; understand how shock is a blockage of other emotions, how loneliness or denial are natural responses, how you might have a tendency to bargain with yourself about how you can get your ex back. Additionally, come to grips with sadness and obsession – how to seek the emotional support or practical support you need to get over your sadness and the habits you can develop to nip obsessive tendencies in your head.

By the end of this book you will be in a position to manage any breakup - no matter how terrible and turbulent - in a healthy, emotionally sensitive way.

Congratulations on taking another step towards moving on from your relationship by reading this book. I trust it will help you on the road to recovery.

1

FOUNDATIONAL ADVICE

Before we talk about how you can learn to manage the specific emotions you are likely to feel during a relationship breakdown and how these emotions progress, it is good to lay down some foundational advice to be mindful of.

1 – Accept your Feelings and your Uniqueness

Firstly, it is important to allow yourself to completely *feel* your feelings. This may sound incredibly obvious and redundant, but many people, when confronted with negative emotional states, struggle to fully accept how they are feeling without resisting, judging these emotions or suppressing them. This leads to these emotional states festering and harming your overall well-being. For an emotion to be dealt with, it needs to be felt intimately, even if this is not a pleasant experience.

Secondly, the emotional response you feel is likely to be unique to you. There are patterns people and psychologists have recognized as typical of individuals who are going through a relationship break-up, but every break-up is different, and so is everyone's response.

You may feel all of the emotions talked about later in this book, few of them, or none of them at all. Some emotions may be overbearingly poignant, whilst others are insignificant. A few emotions may linger for what seems like an eternity, others may only occur in a flash before disappearing entirely. Do not feel obliged to feel a particular way or act to a certain standard that you are trained to expect. The most important aspect of dealing with a relationship is the emotional recovery you undergo in order to be well. If you find yourself in a good place, that's all that matters.

Similarly, there is no 'right' coping method. There are however, a few wrong ones. Try not to self-medicate and develop bad-habits in your attempts to wrestle with your emotions – avoid drinking to excess, or binge eating, substance abuse etc. A few creature comforts can be beneficial to help you curb your initial response, but reliance upon these will ultimately lead to negative outcomes, which in turn could turn a more manageable negative affect into a full-blown depression. Be sensible.

#2 – Seek Support

Another important thing to keep in mind when going through a breakup is to not be afraid to seek support and to take care of ourselves.

Support can come from a variety of ways – talking and spending time with friends or family members, or even joining some support groups of people that are going through similar challenges.

As a small note on seeking social support - it can feel overbearing to be closeted with peers when feeling especially sad, but your friends and family can still help with practical aspects of your day to day life. They can help bring over a healthy meal or a bunch of food supplies, pop-up on occasion. Their offers to lend a hand with housework or talk about the relationship are all ways in which they are showing they care about you. Although it may be difficult to be in the company of others during a breakup, we must not isolate ourselves and ignore those who care about us.

Additionally - If you suspect that the feelings you are experiencing after a break-up are developing into more serious mental health issues, do not be afraid to seek professional help or simply recognize your mental health for what it is. Bouts of depression, as well as a few other issues, are not uncommon after break-ups and you may need to learn to deal with them too. It is nothing to be ashamed of – the only thing that matters here is your well-being!

If need be, take some time off work, but make sure you still arise from your bed in the morning, go out of the house and make sure you're eating properly.

If you don't respect your body's basic needs such as sleep, nutrition and hygiene it can be easy to fall into an unhealthy rut very quickly, where your negative emotional state leads to negative lifestyle habits. Stay active and stay healthy.

Remembering to take care of ourselves and not be scared to seek the support we need is the second step to managing a breakup in a healthy way.

#3 – Remain Civil

Finally, there are a few other points to be made here. Depending on the level of commitment you and your ex shared, you may still need to remain in contact with your former partner in regards to dealings with properties, possessions, family, finances, etc. Even if you are feeling bitter, sad or angry it is important remain civil and agreeable until closure is reached. This will make any contact you have with your ex much more manageable. Holding onto grievances and acting petty can turn small, easy negotiations into full-blown legal disputes, as well as turn necessary formalities into hellish encounters.

Remaining civil with your past partner is the third step in managing a breakup successfully.

2

ALLOW TIME TO PROCESS

With the foundational base to bear in mind, we can now begin to discuss the emotions you are likely to feel – what they are, how you should interpret them and what you can do to manage them.

#4 – Understanding 'Shock'

For many people, especially if the relationship breakdown was unanticipated or sudden, the initial response is shock. You might find yourself asking how the break-up could actually have happened, and be unable to get over the seemingly secure, immutable perception of your relationship that you may have had. This feeling tends to not last for a long duration, but it is important to take steps to manage it, nonetheless.

Shock is an interesting phenomenon because it is most often exhibited as the absence of expected or appropriate response to a situation – often you might be feeling 'nothing'. However, what is actually occurring is that on an intellectual, logical, formal level your mind knows that the relationship you were in is now finished. Yet on an emotional, deeper, more sensitive level your mind is still recoiling from the break-up and taking time to register that you are now single. It is similar in nature to how some people experience grief after the death of a loved one – sometimes it can take several weeks, if not months, for the loss of an individual to be felt. In regards to the demise of your relationship, it too can take time for your grief and loss to become apparent.

The nothingness response that shock creates will often leave people feeling hazy, numb and distracted. It is not quite the full absence of an emotional response but rather the blockage of one – you are not quite ready to feel the emotions waiting to be felt. Shock tends to pass with time, but if you find yourself unable to get past a numb sensation there are a few maneuvers to help.

The most important of these is to gently tease an emotional response from yourself. Think about reasons why the relationship ended, what you can expect from the future or what feelings you think you might be having. Often it takes only a small trigger to release a cascade of emotion allowing you to move on.

The worst thing you can do in regards to shock is to avoid thinking about the event entirely. Your mind needs a small amount of time to process and you can inhibit this by overly distracting yourself or changing your mental dialogue every time the topic of your ex comes. You might need to simply sit down for a while, with no other purpose or responsibilities and allow all your buried emotions to arise – they will, in time.

Allowing yourself the needed time to fully process the shock response you feel is the fourth and vital step in a the road to a healthy breakup.

3

REMAINING OBJECTIVE

#5 – Remain Objective

The ability to keep things in perspective while experiencing the undeniable 'one-sided' emotions throughout the breakup process is a crucial step to managing the ending of a relationship effectively. This chapter will explore some additional emotions we are likely to experience during this process.

Denial

In addition to shock, another emotion many people are prone to experience after a break-up is denial. Denial, like shock, is a similar initial reaction emotion. For relationships that were on and off, or relationships that were frequently marred with difficulty and trouble, it can be easy to deny that the relationship is actually over.

The break-up can be interpreted as just another struggle that will be worked out over time, and the full implication that there is no relationship left to salvage has not been accepted. Denial will often fade over time – but if you find yourself struggling to accept what has happened, just calmly think through the occurrence in your head.

Think about the reasons why the relationship has ended and how you or your ex might have decided to end the relationship. Consider the sincerity in his or hers voice and the realness of the actions that they have taken since. In rare cases it may be possible, after pondering all this, to still think of the relationship as somehow on-going, but for most individuals if they truly allow themselves to process what has occurred, denial will naturally pass.

Bargaining

The tendency to bargain can be interpreted in a way as related to the tendency to deny. Longing for the relationship to continue, an individual who has separated from their ex might start to engage in thinking patterns where they hypothesize that if they are somehow better as an individual, the former relationship might be both rekindled and more feasible.

There a few ways this pattern of thought should be interpreted. Firstly, the viability of maintaining and rekindling the former relationship must be assessed. In some cases, there remains the genuine potential for a former relationship to be restarted in a way that is more beneficial to both parties.

Taking time to separate might lead to a greater calmness and awareness of the faults of both individuals and awaken a true longing to get back together as well as a forgiveness of prior grievances. Ultimately, thinking of ways you can improve the relationship can sometimes be a good think if the relationship can indeed be salvaged.

However, this is not the case for all break-ups. As with denial, consider how the relationship ended. If the break-up was due to both parties needing some distance and the current set-up not working out then perhaps the possibility that the relationship could be started again is feasible. If you have been violently and forcibly ousted by your ex obviously the potential will be less. If there is no potential or mutual willingness for the relationship to start again then bargaining thought patterns are not useful and will prevent you from moving on. You must abandon them.

Recognize Mutual Responsibility

The second thing to consider is the concept of mutual fault – or, another way of looking at it – is mutual responsibility. A romantic relationship is a constant give and take between two people and the collapse of a romantic relationship is likely to be due to the faults and actions of both parties involved.

It can be unhealthy to start to associate the breakdown of the relationship as purely your fault and that if you had just nagged less, or been less aggressive or more outgoing etc., that the relationship would still exist or your partner would return to you. Realize that there are likely to be aspects that both former partners could improve about themselves and aspects that might have struggled to be compatible. Do not take all the blame upon yourself.

Remaining objective and keeping things in perspective is the fifth step in a healthy breakup process.

4

EMOTIONAL INTERPRETATION

Emotional responses that tend to occur later in the emotional progression you may experience or be experiencing will no doubt include sadness, as well as the possibility obsession. Let us consider these in turn.

#6 – Sadness

The most common and the most natural response to any end of a serious romantic relationship – sadness. The strength of the sadness is likely to be proportional to the intensity and meaningfulness of the relationship – you might feel a slight downward tinge or you might feel so intensely unhappy that you actually doubt whether you can achieve happiness again.

When dealing with this type of sadness, remember that it will pass. Often the best antidote is simply time itself - allowing yourself time to grieve the fact that your relationship has ended. Sadness does not always have to be rejected – it is a healthy response to losing something that you are attached to. In addition to this, re-interpret, if you haven't already, the benefits and the advantages of the break-up – the potential to learn life lessons, personal growth, find a more suitable partner and move on to greener pastures. These types of feelings will be discussed later when talking about the feeling of empowerment, but they can be useful to consider here too.

Fully allowing yourself to feel the sadness you experience during a breakup is the sixth and very crucial step of overcoming a breakup effectively.

Obsession

Another emotional response to a break-up might be obsession. You may find in your longing, or even your anger – you are unable to stop thinking about your ex. You might start to wonder what they are doing – whether they seem to be doing better or worse without you, whether they are happy or as unhappy as you are, or any myriad of other thoughts. Ultimately, obsession in this context is characterized as an unhealthy, prolonged and fixated interest in a person that you are no longer romantically involved with.

Obsession is one of the more dangerous emotional responses that you can experience and it needs to be recognized and dealt with as such. Other emotional states tend to be unpleasant (i.e. sadness) or work themselves out over time (e.g. denial or shock). Obsession however, by its very nature, does not want to forget the object it is obsessed with, and if you are obsessed with something, you will likely greatly resist steps to further separate yourself from it.

To help prevent or manage obsessive tendencies, it is often best to go completely without any sort of stimulus reminders of your ex. Avoid your social media accounts if you know that your ex will be inevitably displayed in your feed – or try to eliminate your ex's presence on your social media by removing him or her from your friends list. Similarly, make sure you delete their phone number from your mobile and get rid of other means of contact (unless, of course, you must remain in contact for whatever reason).

In a similar vein, put away photos or objects with sentimental value, somewhere where they are not in immediate sight. In time you can learn to either dissociate the presence of your ex with those items, or not find their presence as salient, but for now you probably need to just give yourself some metaphorical distance from them.

Lastly, when dealing with obsession, try to be mindful of your thought patterns. Distract yourself, or engage in something that captures your attention when you start to dwell and obsess over your ex. Simply having strong and fulfilling hobbies to throw yourself into can be a great way to do this – if you don't have any strong hobbies that come to mind then right now can be a great opportunity to try some new activities.

5

RE-INTERPRETING FEAR

Another major emotion you are susceptible to experiencing during a relationship break-up is fear.

#7 – Fear

In regards to fear, this can manifest itself in multiple ways. People in long-term relationships often identify themselves with their partner – they only feel whole as an individual by the presence of their other half. Owing to this, when these kinds of individuals become bereft from their partner they suffer from a loss of identity, which can be frightening.

Additionally, fear may manifest itself as a kind of uncertainty that taints beliefs that you were previously confident in. Romantic partners experience a kind of unique intimacy – a surrendering of oneself, a giving of trust and warmth to another person. Depending on the type of relationship, people might also perceive the other individual as a soul mate, as *the one*. Having this kind of perception broken by the relationship failing can lead to lack of confidence in other beliefs that seemed secure. It can also lead to an unwillingness to commit to or trust future feelings of intimacy.

Finally, fear can also occur due to the thought of trying to cope with the world alone. Often, in a relationship, the burden of managing your day to day life is shared and made easier by having a partner to confide in and hold your hand through the difficulties.

When you realize you will have to navigate turbulent waters alone and this can be very intimidating. It is important to recognize your own competency here – in most circumstance, realize that you managed fine enough on your own before the relationship began – managing your finances, your lifestyle, even your day-to-day chores and responsibility.

Even if you were more reliant on your partner – in the sense that they either helped you develop your own inner strength or perhaps supported you in more explicit ways – realize how you have developed as a person and your own capabilities. People are generally more resilient and tougher than they believe – having a little faith in yourself, that you can deal with the world by yourself will go a long way in soothing that burning fear you may be experiencing.

Furthermore, know that you are often not alone – friends, family, even support groups exist to help you get back on your feet and discover your own confidence.

In a more general sense, there is the feeling that you are taking a new venture alone – and with new waters come uncertainty and doubt (which may cause fear). It may be necessary to re-establish yourself as a solitary individual. When you are feeling afraid, instead of backing down, slowly build yourself up – doing more activities that require greater amounts of confidence will eventually leaving yourself feeling whole.

Addressing your fear and re-establishing yourself as a solitary, complete individual is the seventh step to overcoming a breakup in an emotionally intelligent way.

6

A RENEWED OUTLOOK

#8 – Liberation and Acceptance

The final emotions that need to be discussed are liberation and empowerment. Ending a non-beneficial relationship need not even induce negative emotion!

Instead it can be incredibly empowering – it can be an opportunity to take control of your life and address the problems within it. Furthermore, in a way related to the last point, it is also vouching for the confidence and strength within yourself – that you will be fine without the relationship in your life.

This realization can be incredibly potent. In addition to this, the entire experience can be taken as a learning curve – even though the relationship did not work out, you are still in a better position for having been in the relationship because now you have learned several life lessons. Perhaps you now know what qualities and traits you value in a partner, or what qualities and traits you simply are not compatible with.

Similarly, on all the other issues that might relate to a relationship – work, finance, family, hobbies, etc. you now have a more refined stance on what you are looking for and how to manage them. Perhaps now you know that you want to achieve a certain life goal before entering a new relationship, or simply go more slowly, etc.

#9 – Empowerment

Empowerment is another great sign in your emotional progression of the relationship ending; it signals a great deal of acceptance – you no longer cling to the relationship and either secretly aim to rekindle it or grieve hopelessly for its loss. Instead you have come to terms with the break-up – no matter how painful – and now you are ready, if not already, moving on.

Additionally, there is a wondrous feeling of excitement and freedom that can occur here – you are no longer shackled in a painful and broken relationship and you can now go on to seek more fertile soils and genuinely improve your life. There is nothing holding you back. As common folk logic dictates, as one thing ends another thing begins. Every cloud has a silver lining – a new and better future can grow from the ashes of the memories of your ex.

Developing a renewed outlook on life — truly accepting the present situation and discovering your inner liberation and empowerment - are the final steps in coming to terms with the fact that one particular relationship in your life has come to a close and that new ones may begin.

CONCLUSION

Thank you again for reading.

I trust this book was able to aid you in the process of managing with a relationship break-up, often one of the most taxing and trying periods in your life. The emotional fallout from long-term, serious relationships can last not just weeks, but months and years. Some people can get stuck in place, unable to move on in a healthy manner. This can seriously affect the other achievements people look forward to in life – moving forward in their careers, their personal goals and even seeking other partners.

Breakups can also lead people to act in ways that they will later come to regret – isolating themselves from friends, being rude and aggressive to their ex, making moving out and negotiations difficult as well as developing bad habits that can last a lifetime.

However, by having read this guide, you are now in a better position than before to deal with any break-up with grace and speed, avoiding the common pitfalls. You should now be in touch with your emotions and know how to be mindful of them and manage them skillfully. You now know the characteristic emotional responses – shock, sadness, obsession, denial, empowerment what they mean, how to interpret them and how you should respond. You now understand that the emotional responses you experience after a breakdown follow a certain path – a path that is unique to you, but often shares features of how other people respond.

All that there is left for you to do is to go on with your life, moving forward positively and constructively, to further happiness and love.

SHARE YOUR EXPERIENCE

Finally, if you enjoyed or benefited from this book, then I would like to ask you for a favor:

Would you be kind enough to leave a review for this book on Amazon?

Share the tools and techniques to help others effectively come to terms with their relationship closure and help others move on to the path or acceptance and a renewed sense of living.

Visit Amazon.com and search 'BreakUp Brittany Hallison' to be brought to the book's page in which you can leave your feedback.

Thank you, and best wishes with moving on to more fulfilling and enriching relationships.

BONUS EXCERPT

LETTING GO:
Surrender, Release Attachments and
Accept the Present

We are all aware that we cling to negative thought patterns and habits. We obsess over how we look, even though deep down we know that judgments based on our appearances are shallow and meaningless. We stress over our responsibilities all the time, even though life carries on whether we do the housework or not. We become unhappy if our relationships are not fruitful or if people around us do not celebrate or revere our presence.

Most other books in the western world promise that if we can just improve ourselves, we can be happier. We just need to be a little more disciplined, a little fitter and a little smarter. It doesn't matter that we already seem exhausted and overwhelmed by the chaos and demands of modern life; others suggest we need to do more and be more.

This book, however, offers a different approach. The solution to all our stresses and anxieties and the key to true happiness is letting go of all our needless attachments. If we let go of our need to be beautiful, we do not let that stubborn facial acne or that dry skin ruin our day. If we let go of the desire for everyone to like us, we do not become frustrated when people do not. If we let go of the need for the house to be spotless, we can focus on what genuinely matters in our lives. We don't have to become careless about our appearance, let our houses become a mess or be rude to others - but we don't need to let these aspects of our lives cause ourselves suffering either. We just need to be.

The teachings discussed here will give you the knowledge and understanding needed to start letting go of all your harmful attachments. We will begin by first discussing the reasons and importance of *why* you need to let go of pointless and harmful attachments, by delving into a little Buddhist philosophy and eastern thought. You will read and understand about *how* you can start to let go and live a happier life. Finally, you will be given practical and down-to-earth advice about small changes you can make to your life to be happier and let go of your attachments, brought about by your new understanding of 'letting go'.

You have already taken the first step towards letting go and living a more fulfilled life. I trust you will greatly benefit from the teachings.

Chapter 1

Most of us would have heard about 'letting go' of our attachments at some point in our lives. Even if we don't know enough about the eastern philosophies from where this advice originates, many of us see the wisdom in letting things go. We all tend to be aware that we have habits that cause us pain; negative thinking patterns and unhelpful desires and attachments that may cause us to fret over the future or feel shameful about the past.

However, almost no-one offers advice on *how* to let go of the various attachments that are hurting us. We are constantly told that letting go helps us on a spiritual journey, but no-one ever provides directions or points out the landmarks. Surely, if letting go needed no instruction than none of us would be in the predicament where we attach to harmful thoughts. Yet we all are, at least to some degree.

This chapter aims to rectify this lack of instruction and knowledge. In particular, this chapter will provide an exploration of the philosophies behind the mantra of 'letting go'. We will briefly cover Buddhism and how letting go relates to attachment and other Buddhist principles. Next, we will explore the topic of letting go in more detail; what it actually means to let go and how we can teach ourselves to let go of harmful aspects of our everyday lives. In essence, this chapter will discuss *what* letting go actually means and *why* you should let go.

In the following chapters, we will explore topics such as *how* to let go as well as the actions and perspectives we need to embrace in our lives to rid ourselves or unhelpful desires.

Mindset

To learn how to let go involves a multi-faceted approach. In the following chapters we will discuss some of the practical aspects of letting go; this chapter concerns itself with letting go from a more spiritual and philosophical perspective.

In the Buddhist tradition, letting go has been explained like dropping a hot object. Letting go isn't an action we consciously do; we cannot let go of our attachments with a switch of a mental button or through meditation - or whatever means we imagine. Rather, truly letting go is more of an instinct.

It is a deep realization that our attachments and desires are hurting us. If we were to clumsily pick up a scolding hot object, our innate reflexes would cause us to realize the object is hurting us and drop it. Letting go is like realizing we are actually holding on to that scolding painful attachment; we can then drop that attachment without a second thought.

Experiential Understanding

This realization may be easy to understand conceptually, however actually internalizing this understanding experientially involves much more skill and practice. Eastern philosophies talk about different levels of knowledge and the difference between knowing something intellectually and knowing something on a deeper, spiritual level.

All of us, at some point in our lives have had times where a concept or idea has just 'clicked'. We may have understood the idea, such as an opposing viewpoint or an academic theory, but we couldn't understand the value of the idea.

Then, at some point, perhaps when we were actively thinking about the idea, or perhaps at some random trigger, something in our minds change. We suddenly open up to the idea in a way we previously didn't imagine. Perhaps we see it in a slightly different light or perhaps it just becomes salient and meaningful in a way it wasn't before. We have a slight epiphany; we begin to understand on a deeper level.

It is this understanding that is required to truly let go. We may often believe that we are not attached to good looks, food, wealth, money, relationships and more but our behavior and actions betray us. It is only through this deeper realization that letting go actually occurs.

This perspective might seem to force us into an unsolvable quandary; we understand that we need to let go of certain aspects of our lives, but we cannot directly force ourselves to let go. However, the solution is to try and make ourselves let go through both direct and indirect methods.

To read the rest of *Letting Go* simply visit Amazon.com and search 'Letting Go Brittany Hallison' to view the available book editions. This book is available in e-book, audiobook and paperback format.

OTHER WORKS BY B. L. HALLISON

Meditation for Beginners: How to Meditate to Relieve Stress, Anxiety and Depression and Live Peacefully

Mindfulness for Beginners: Relieve Stress, Live Worry-Free and Cure Anxiety with Mindfulness Meditation

The Complete Guide to YOGA: Yoga for Beginners, Yoga for Weight Loss, Yoga Poses, Benefits and More

Social Anxiety Cure: Relieve Social Anxiety, Overcome Shyness and Be Confident for Life

The Procrastination Cure: The Ultimate Solution Guide on How to Overcome Procrastination and Develop Practical Time Management Strategies for Life

Interview and Get Any Job You Want: Employment Techniques and How to Answer Toughest Interview Questions

A Beginner's Guide to Internet Marketing: 17 Proven Online Marketing Strategies to Make Money Online and Grow Your Online Business

Facebook Marketing: 25 Best Strategies on Using Facebook for Advertising, Business and Making Money Online

Social Media Domination: Social Media Marketing Strategies with Facebook, Twitter, YouTube, Instagram and Linked In

Chronic Fatigue Syndrome Solution: Overcome and Cure Chronic Fatigue Syndrome Using Effective Recovery and Treatment Methods

All books are currently offered in e-book format, and many are also available in paperback and audio-book editions as well.

Visit Brittany's author page at: **amazon.com/author/brittanyhallison** to see available options.

ABOUT THE AUTHOR

Brittany L. Hallison has always loved reading and writing from a very young age. She has always felt that through books, she is able to make a stronger sense of connection with others - be it with characters, writers or the information itself.

Brittany writes about a wide range of topics including personal growth and development, spirituality and internal health and wellness. More recently, she has also expanded her writing to working with other authors and contributing to book topics such as online marketing and business.

Brittany strives to write about things in which she feels can contribute to others. Her books always aim to offer a source of information, inspiration, reassurance and method to overcome a challenge or problem they are encountering. Nothing is more rewarding to a writer then being able to help people and make a difference in their lives.

"The pen is indeed mightier than the sword."

Made in the USA
San Bernardino, CA
18 December 2016